Colonial Voices
Hear Them Speak

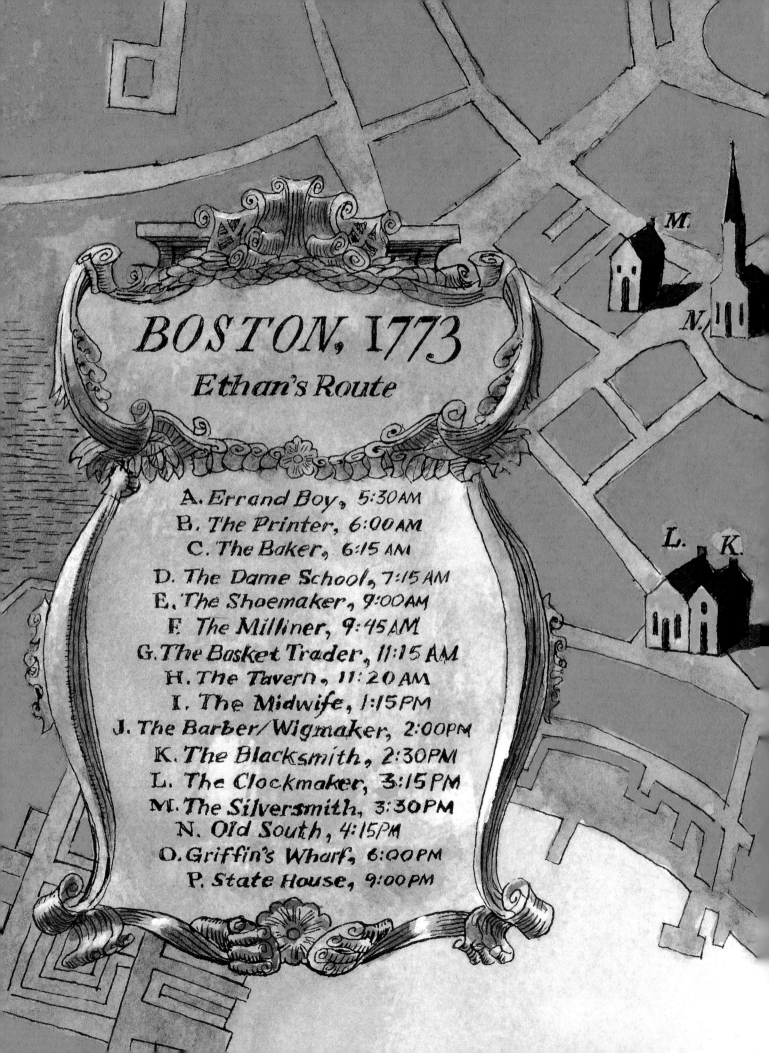

BOSTON, 1773
Ethan's Route

A. Errand Boy, 5:30AM
B. The Printer, 6:00AM
C. The Baker, 6:15 AM
D. The Dame School, 7:15 AM
E. The Shoemaker, 9:00AM
F. The Milliner, 9:45AM
G. The Basket Trader, 11:15 AM
H. The Tavern, 11:20AM
I. The Midwife, 1:15PM
J. The Barber/Wigmaker, 2:00PM
K. The Blacksmith, 2:30PM
L. The Clockmaker, 3:15PM
M. The Silversmith, 3:30PM
N. Old South, 4:15PM
O. Griffin's Wharf, 6:00PM
P. State House, 9:00PM

KAY WINTERS

Colonial Voices
HEAR THEM SPEAK

illustrated by LARRY DAY

PUFFIN BOOKS
An Imprint of Penguin Group (USA)

To Stephanie Lurie, a phenomenal editor
To my husband, Earl, I couldn't do it without you
—K.W.

To Esther Hershenhorn, an inspiration to us all
—L.D.

The author would like to acknowledge Michele leBlanc, Education Director at Old South Meeting House, for reviewing the manuscript. Thanks to Sheila Cooke-Keyser, Education Specialist, Boston National Historical Park, for answering my questions, and the staff at the David Library of the American Revolution and the Massachusetts Historical Society, who helped me locate appropriate research materials.

I am especially appreciative of writer friends who provided helpful insights—Esther Hershenhorn, Deborah Heiligman, Sally Keehn, Elvira Woodruff, Laurie Anderson, Pat Brisson, Joyce McDonald, Pam Swallow, Martha Hewson, Wendy Pfeffer, Susan Korman, Ruth Radin, Marilyn Hazelton, Pat Goodrich, Sandra Feder, Susan Weaver, Allison Lassieur, and Karen Huang.   K.W.

PUFFIN BOOKS
Published by the Penguin Group
Penguin Group (USA) LLC
375 Hudson Street
New York, New York 10014

USA * Canada * UK * Ireland * Australia
New Zealand * India * South Africa * China

penguin.com
A Penguin Random House Company

First published in the United States of America by Dutton Children's Books,
a division of Penguin Young Readers Group, 2008
Published by Puffin Books, an imprint of Penguin Young Readers Group, 2015

Text copyright © 2008 by Kay Winters
Illustrations copyright © 2008 by Larry Day

THE LIBRARY OF CONGRESS HAS CATALOGED THE DUTTON CHILDREN'S BOOKS EDITION AS FOLLOWS:
Winters, Kay.
Colonial voices: hear them speak / by Kay Winters ; illustrated by Larry Day
p. cm. Includes bibliographical references.
ISBN 978-0-525-47872-0 (hardcover)
1. Boston Tea Party, 1773—Juvenile literature. 2. Boston (Mass.)—History—Revolution,
1775–1783—Juvenile literature. 3. United States—History—Revolution,
1775–1783—Causes—Juvenile literature.
I. Day, Larry, date. II. Title. E215.7.W63 2008 973.3'115—dc22 2007028480

Puffin Books ISBN 978-0-14-751162-1

Designed by Jason Henry

Printed in the United States of America

·THE· ERRAND BOY

TODAY IS DECEMBER 16, 1773.
Boston is about to explode!

I'm Ethan,
paperboy for the printer,
messenger, woodchopper, runner of errands.
My mother died when I was born.
My father drowned at sea.

Now I sleep above the print shop,
live by my wits.
No one times my comings and goings.
Errand boys, like servants, are almost invisible.
It's a good cloak to wear.
I keep my eyes and ears alert,
and trouble's brewing.

The *Dartmouth*, the *Eleanor*, the *Beaver*,
crammed with tea,
wait at Griffin's wharf.

Will King George and Parliament have their way?
Will their custom men collect the tax?
Will the tea company say who sells the tea?

LET THEM TRY!

The Sons of Liberty are counting on me.
Off I go to slip in and out of shops and houses,
share the notice about the final meeting at Old South,
pass the secret to the Patriots,
and listen to the tittle-tattle from the Loyalists.

Midnight is the deadline
when the tea must go or be taxed.

What will happen now?

· THE · PRINTER

I AM THE PRINTER.
My job is to keep folks informed.
I write, edit, compose the type,
operate the press.
When my husband and I opened our small shop,
news of the King's birthday, missing cows,
runaway slaves, filled our paper.
How times have changed!

I am a widow now, but I keep the press rolling.
First Parliament passed the Stamp Act,
then British soldiers occupied our town.
Citizens were shot. I told each tale.

Now Parliament and King George the III
have done it again.
The terrible Tea Act.
Taxes to pay without any say.

UNFAIR, cry the Patriots.
But what do the Loyalists want,
and those who are in-between?

I've done my part.
Published the paper,
printed the notice of today's meeting.

Governor Hutchinson
is the one who must decide
whether the tea ships stay or go.

What will the governor do?

· THE · BAKER

THE BIG BRICK OVEN HEATS THE ROOM
until we swelter,
but bakes the bread with thickened crusts
the town folk crave.

I sift flour into a wooden trough and stir the batch.
My apprentice kneads a hundred pounds
with burly arms and practiced hands.
Slowly, the dough bubbles and rises.
"Like liberty," I say.

Here's Ethan,
making his rounds.
He hands me a notice
and shares the secret from the Sons of Liberty.

"King George may be surprised
by what we do...." I wink, and
give the boy a loaf to feed him on his way.

The apprentice sweeps the ashes from the oven floor.
I slide new loaves in on my wooden peel,
shut the iron door, and close the damper.
As darkness fades from morning sky,
a yeasty smell perfumes the air.

A new day.
Fresh bread for sale!

·THE MISTRESS OF THE·
DAME SCHOOL

THE KITCHEN IS MY SCHOOLROOM.
When sun is up the children come
to do their lessons.

They join my Charlotte, Paul, and baby Benjamin.
Abigail and Daniel bring firewood, part of my pay.
Matthew, John, and Hannah have hornbooks round their necks.

I start the day by reading from the Bible.
Then we say rhymes to learn the letters *A* to *Z*.
Paul's face turns red when we all chant:

> *F—Fool —The Idle Fool*
> *Is Whipt at School.*

Yesterday he poked Daniel during spelling.
I didn't whip him,
but I made him wear the whispering sticks all afternoon.

Who comes?
IT'S ETHAN——WITH NEWS ABOUT TODAY!
I ask the scholars
to repeat the time and place.

Back to our books.
We read aloud.
Abigail knows the words! We clap.
My heart sings.
A special day—were it not for those three tea ships
lurking in the harbor.
King George does not give up.
But nor do we.

·THE· SHOEMAKER

CUSTOMERS CROWD MY SHOP.
Walking wears soles thin.
I never want for work.

I measure the length of the foot,
whittle the wooden *last*,
mark it with my customer's name.

Two pieces of leather make the upper,
one for the toe and one for the heel.
I punch holes in the top
for leather string or silver buckles,
then cut and stitch the sole.
Left or right I make the same.
The wearer switches every day.

Sometimes I pull a throbbing tooth
for him who has an aching mouth.
An extra charge!
But always I listen as I work.

I do not share my views.
Don't want to lose my customers who differ.
But times are changing.
THIS TEA TAX MUST NOT BE PAID.

Meeting today?

My teeth are worn from so much clenching.
Mayhap the time has come to take a stand.

· T H E · MILLINER

I SELL THE LATEST FRIPPERIES IN MY SHOP—
lace, fans, hats, velvet shoes, a scarlet cloak,
silk flowers, fabric, beaded purses, muffs, and mitts.
Ladies look to me for fashion
in these troubled times.

I can make old look new
by dyeing silk from pink to red.
Or freshen last year's gown
by rubbing stains with bread.
My ladies ask . . .

This season, will the petticoat show?
The shoe buckles twinkle with gems?
Are cuffs of lace, a nosegay at the waist
what stylish women wear in England or in France?

And once the Patriots come to their senses,
my customers will sip tea in fragile cups
while they chitter-chatter over shapes of skirts.

"What did you say? Another meeting at Old South
about that tiny tax?"

I say, "PAY IT! Count your blessings.
I prefer the King to a rabble-rousing mob!"
No meeting for me or any of my kin.
We'll be unpacking pretties for the shop.

·THE·
BASKET
TRADER

MY ANCESTORS AND I WERE HERE FOR MANY MOONS
before strangers stepped upon our shores.
They bring sickness
we cannot cure,
make promises they do not keep.

They turn our trails into roads
for carriages and carts,
claim land, plant fields,
build cities and towns.

They shoot our fowl,
catch our fish,
stalk our hunting ground,
force us to move on.

Now they quarrel with each other
like warring tribes,
and over tea!
We will not fight their battle.
It matters not who wins or loses.

OUR PEOPLE HAVE ALREADY LOST.

I do not live in town,
but come and go to the tavern
to help make soap or candles.
I barter willow baskets
for kettles, needles, knives.
My moccasins walk between two worlds.
I pray I will not stumble.

·THE· TAVERN KEEPER

SINCE MY HUSBAND DIED,
I am mistress of this place.
I cannot let my sorrow show;
a gloomy landlady loses custom.

I smile and take the traveler
up the stairs
to see the bed he'll share with strangers.

My daughter serves the table
where guests gather.
They toast the King,
sit, sup, then share their views.
They bring the news from whence they've come.

The town folk tarry, read the paper,
talk of tea, taxes, and today.
I won't be there.

"We should be thankful
to get that English tea!" I say.
"SUCH A TEMPEST!"

I check the chicken,
stir the soup, taste the turnips,
prod the cook, clean the counter,
plan the menu.
My husband taught me well.
Cash is what I take for bed and board.
Trust is not the innkeeper's friend.

I've trusted
many, to my
sorrow.
Pay today,
I'll trust
tomorrow.

· THE · MIDWIFE

ETHAN CAME TO FETCH ME,
for the coming of new life.
I brew tea from sage and chamomile
to calm Mistress Church
and her sister, who paces by the bed.
Eight hundred sixty babes have I brought forth without a mishap
(though I mourn the ones I've lost).

The father sits at the Green Dragon
plotting with the Sons of Liberty.
The mother moans.
It's time.
I send the sister for the neighbors to assist me,
hold the mother's hand, say soothing words.
The babe tarries just an hour before his head appears.

At last! The child is come.
"Matthew," the mother murmurs.
I spank his bottom to hear his cry.
He blinks his eyes against the bright new world,

A TINY PATRIOT!

What will his future be?
        My heart fills;
                my eyes spill.

We women gather by the bed and offer thanks.
My payment, a yard of ribbon
and baby pig, does not tell the tale
of why I am a midwife.

·THE· BARBER/ WIGMAKER

IN MY SHOP I SOAP AND SHAVE
the heads and chins of clients.
These days only pirates wear beards.

Unlike the blacksmith, my hands keep clean,
except when I let blood to cure a fever
or place a leech to ease a blackened eye.

Last week, the judge stopped to choose his wig.
I shaved his head and measured.
My journeyman sorted, cleaned, and baked
the last of the human hair from London,
the best quality to be had!

Holding back on English goods
is bad for business.
PAY THE TEA TAX AND MOVE ON!
But I'll not share my views today
with that rowdy crowd.

My journeyman combs hair through the hackle.
I weave the strands in rows and stitch them to a cap.
No goat's or horse's hair for this important sir!
The wig's perfumed, then sprinkled well with powder.

The judge returns to have his fitting,
I place the wig just so.
    I stop. . . admire.

      He looks a proper Englishman!

·THE· BLACKSMITH'S SLAVE

I WAS SEIZED IN AFRICA,
thrown on a ship,
shaken, beaten, branded.

When we landed,
the captain sold me
to the highest bidder.

My master is a blacksmith.
We make axes, andirons, hinges, hooks,
padlocks, pokers, latches, and nails,
thousands of nails.

I fill the forge, pull the bellows, and stir the coals.
The master is old.
He needs my muscle.
I heat the iron, lift it from the forge.
My master strikes and shapes it on the anvil.

Men sit in his shop and talk of tea,
taxes, liberty, and freedom.

FREEDOM FOR THEM, BUT NOT FOR ME.

I am a slave.
I will always be bound.

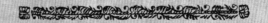

·THE· CLOCKMAKER

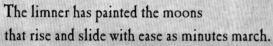

I HEAR TIME PASSING IN MY SHOP.
    Tick……… Tock….
    Tick……… Tock….
Change is in the air.
My pendulums click the seconds
on grandfather clocks of such quality
that only fine gentlemen can buy.

The limner has painted the moons
that rise and slide with ease as minutes march.
    Tick……… Tock….
    Tick……… Tock….

But some of my clocks, the wag-on-the-walls,
have just one hand.
They mark the hour for ordinary folk,
who earn the right to know the time
as much as wealthy neighbors.
No fancy case to raise the cost,
just the face and my well-made works.

My weight cords
        d
        a
        n
        g
        l
        e
      f r e e
    as we long to be.

Here's Ethan!
I read the notice and hear the secret about tonight.
I fetch a blanket and collect some soot.
I'm ready!
Change *is* in the air.
    The time has come!

·THE· SILVERSMITH'S APPRENTICE

WHEN MY FATHER DIED, THERE WAS NO KIN TO KEEP ME.
I was apprenticed to the silversmith, who had no son.
The master vowed to feed me,
house me, teach me to read and write.

He keeps his word
and shows me the secrets of his trade.
Till I turn twenty-one my labors are his due,
but I feel like family.

He is a Patriot, with skills so fine the Loyalists care not,
and I support his cause of public liberty.

WE WILL NOT PAY WHEN WE'VE HAD NO SAY.

Tonight we'll make our mark.
Ethan's shared the notices
and spread the secret to those who need to know.
We will be heard.

I sweep the shop, heat the crucible to melt the coins,
watch my master pound his hammers,
make silver smooth as silk.

Someday I'll be the one to sketch the teapot, etch the picture,
turn the handle.
My hours are many; my pay is nil, but I learn my craft.
I do not curse my fate.
I could have been a stableboy who mucks manure.
To work with silver is to make shapes that shine.

We shut the shop and hurry to Old South.

·A SON OF· LIBERTY

MY APPRENTICE AND I
crowd into the back of Old South Meeting House.
Thousands of colonists from Boston town
and nearby villages
fill every seat, stand on the side, linger in the street,
wait to hear the fate of the tea.

Tonight our weeks of work
will tell the tale.
Will the governor grant permission
for the tea ships to sail back to England
with the cargo still on board?
I think not!

In Old South, candles are lit against the darkening day.
Sam Adams and Joseph Warren rouse the crowd.
Josiah Quincy urges caution.
The *Dartmouth*'s owner hurries in at last.
His face sags with sorry news.
The governor will not agree.
The tea must stay, the tax be paid.

"NAY!" roars the crowd. "NAY!!!!"
Sam Adams stands up and pounds the gavel.

"THIS MEETING CAN DO NO MORE TO SAVE THE COUNTRY."

War whoops sound.
"Boston Harbor is a teapot tonight!" shouts one.
"Who knows how tea will mingle with salt water?" cries another.
"To Griffin's wharf!" I shout.
"To the wharf!" roars the crowd.

·MORE THAN AN· ERRAND BOY

A T LAST!
  The secret's out.
We're standing up to the Crown,
and I helped make it happen!
I run to the blacksmith's shop,
streak my face with soot,
wrap my blanket like a "Mohawk,"
dash to the *Dartmouth*, and climb aboard.

The rain has stopped.
Lanterns light the deck.
Thunk! Splat!
The "warriors" and I split wooden boxes
while the captain and his crew stand by.
Thunk! Splat!
We ax the lids,
then spill the tea and heave the heavy chests.
The tea leaves float.
Thousands watch from the wharf.
They wait in silence.
On British warships docked nearby,
no sailor sounds a warning.

·THE· PATRIOTS

WE ARE JOURNEYMEN, APPRENTICES, MERCHANTS,
  who worked side by side,
speaking out for liberty.
We boarded the *Dartmouth*, the *Eleanor*, the *Beaver*
and dumped the tea,
though many Loyalists disagreed.
The deed is done!

We clamber down from the decks
and shake our shoes.
"What a cup of tea we made for the fishes,"
says a "Mohawk."

We fall into ranks.
Up through town we march
out of the range of British guns.
As we near the State House,
our spirits soar, our steps are brisk.
We keep time to the fifer's tune.

No harm to crew or ships.
No paying tax on tea,
no bowing to the King.

We said NAY
and held a party.
A tea party.

WHAT WILL HAPPEN NOW?

· HISTORICAL NOTES ·

The colonial period in American history took place during the seventeenth and eighteenth centuries when immigrants from Europe, slaves from Africa, and Native Americans inhabited the thirteen colonies. Ethan and his role in the Boston Tea Party are fictional. Hear the re-created voices of a milliner, baker, midwife, printer, school mistress, tavern owner, shoemaker, and others whose occupations and political beliefs played a significant role in the colonies. The Boston Tea Party was held in response to the Tea Act, passed by the British Parliament, which granted the East India Company a monopoly for providing tea, and permitted the company to choose who would sell the tea. In addition, colonists were to pay a tea tax. In 1773 there were colonists who were Patriots, Loyalists, and in-betweens living in Boston. The Patriots wanted the freedoms that British citizens enjoyed, and eventually independence. The Loyalists felt that the King was their ruler and colonists should obey British rule. The in-betweens were neutral or could see both sides. The tea meetings began on Monday, December 13, and continued through December 16, with the grand finale occurring after 5:00 P.M. The Sons of Liberty and the Committee of Correspondence played a major role in organizing the rebellion.

THE ERRAND BOY

Young boys of eleven or twelve often ran errands for merchants or householders. They worked in households, stables, on the docks, at the mill, or did various unskilled tasks for merchants in exchange for food, board, or small amounts of money. They differed from apprentices, who were taught a skill in exchange for room and board and were bound to their masters for a specific number of years.

THE PRINTER

By 1732 there were print shops in most large cities in the colonies. Several of the shops were run or owned by women. In the larger shops, apprentices and journeymen took on the tasks of setting the type and running the press. In small shops the work was done by one person. Print shops produced pamphlets, books, handbills, legal forms, and broadsides. But their most important service was the newspaper, which kept colonists informed of current events and provided merchants with a place to advertise their goods and services. Newspapers were carried from colony to colony by travelers and post riders. Citizens in North Carolina could read about what was happening in Philadelphia or Boston. As competition grew, papers with Patriot or Loyalist leanings were pitted against each other, sometimes resulting in destruction of a particular print shop. The newspapers, pamphlets, and broadsides roused the indignation of many colonists against the laws and restrictions imposed by England and played a starring role in the quest for independence.

THE BAKER

By the 1700s, bakeries could be found in every town in the colonies large enough to boast a tavern. Millers provided the baker with milled flour, and rye or white loaves were baked in brick ovens. The baker added more flour to the "sponge," a thin dough made of warm water, yeast, flour, and mashed potatoes. The sponge was kept going daily. In the South, bread was baked on the premises of plantations, though in towns like Annapolis, Maryland, and Williamsburg, Virginia, bread could be bought in bakeshops. The bakers wore hats to keep the flour from covering their hair. Customers brought a napkin or cloth to carry the bread home. The baker's wife or children usually sold the bread in the shop.

THE SCHOOL MISTRESS

Young children in the North-ern colonies went to a dame school held in a woman's home. Students learned reading, writ-ing, and simple sums, although arithmetic texts were scarce. A common school or writing school was also available for older students in large towns. Those teachers were men and the students mostly boys. There were a few boarding schools for young ladies. Children in the South were often tutored by a minister. In all the schools the students read reli-gious texts and were expected to obey the teacher. A widely used textbook was *The New England Primer*. Discipline was strict. Slave children, for the most part, received no schooling.

THE SHOEMAKER

The first shoemaker arrived in New England in 1629. He was called a cordwainer. Walking was a major means of transportation for many colonists, so shoemakers were in high demand. At first Bos-ton was where the majority settled, but by 1721, there were several hundred shoemakers in New York. Chil-dren's shoes were made two sizes too large. Children wrapped their feet in cloth until they grew into their shoes. In the middle colonies customers brought in their own leather. In the South, the shoemaker made shoes for slaves, but plantation owners often imported footwear for their families from England. The shoe-maker's shop was a social place where men discussed political issues while their shoes were made or re-paired.

THE MILLINER

When we think of the milliner, we often think of hats. But hats were not the only item that decked her shop. Fabrics, shoes, jewelry, lace, gloves, and dishes were imported from England, France, and Italy. She also sold tobacco, handkerchiefs, stockings, and neckwear for men. The milliner displayed dolls dressed in the latest styles for her customers to admire and order a similar gown. Some milli-ners employed mantua makers. These seamstresses designed and fit each dress to the customer. If the lady could not come to the shop, the mantua maker would go to the customer's home. Most milliners were women.

THE BASKET TRADER

The arrival of the colonists had a significant impact on Native Americans, or Indians as they were called. Some lived outside the big towns and survived by making and selling baskets, trading goods, and doing odd jobs. They lost many members to European diseases that they had no immunity to combat. Tribal interest in the war between the English and the Ameri-cans had to do with independence—Indian indepen-dence.

THE TAVERN KEEPER

Taverns were important gathering places in the colonies. The town council only issued licenses to re-spected citizens. During the eighteenth century, the tavern was a meeting place, a news exchange, a mail drop, a courtroom, a place to socialize, and also offered bed and board to travelers. Sizzling political discus-sions took place. Patrons of some taverns favored the Patriots, others the Loyalists, and some custom-ers were neutral. The Green Dragon in Boston is said to be where the planning of the Tea Party took place. Auctions of slaves, orphans, paupers, and goods took place in taverns. Turtle frolics, catfish feasts, and shad suppers were community events. Foxhunts, cockfights and bullbaiting were organized for enter-tainment. Women often became landlords when their husbands died.

THE MIDWIFE

Midwives were plentiful in all the colonies, as were the number of babies they delivered. A South Carolina newspaper reported that Elizabeth Hunt had brought nearly four thousand infants into the world. Most midwives had multiple duties. Besides helping with births, they ground medicines, prepared the dead for burial, and nursed people who were ill. Women advertised their services in the newspaper. On a plantation, female slaves frequently provided midwife services to whites as well as blacks.

THE BARBER/WIGMAKER

The barber was a person of many talents. He/she cut hair, shaved chins and heads, prepared wigs and cleaned them. In the North the barber was sometimes called upon to let blood in the hope of reducing infection, and to use leeches for bruises. The wig craze started in the late 1600s in France, spread to England and America, and was in full swing in the 1700s. Both men and women wore wigs. The wigs came in various colors and styles. If the hair for the wig refused to curl, the barber would send it on curlers to the baker to be enclosed in a loaf of rye bread and baked. The wig fad faded after the Revolution.

THE BLACKSMITH/ THE SLAVE

Slaves were often taught the blacksmith trade in both the North and South. Those who were bound to artisans became involuntary apprentices and were considered the property of their owners. For most slaves there was no end to bondage. By 1775, blacks made up a fifth of the population in the American colonies. The blacksmith was one of the most essential craftsmen in colonial days. Colonists like the cabinetmaker, the wheelwright, the gunsmith, and the carriage maker were dependent on his services. The blacksmith made and repaired the tools they needed to ply their crafts. He was the only person who could repair guns used by the militia to defend the colonies. In the South most plantations required their own blacksmith, and slaves often provided this service.

THE CLOCKMAKER

The first grandfather clock, sometimes called a tall clock or coffin clock, is believed to have been made by Benjamin Bagnall in New England. But only wealthy citizens could afford to buy clocks. In the early 1700s, clockmakers set up shops in all the major cities of the colonies. The wag-on-the-wall was made from the inner works of the grandfather clock and could be mounted on a bracket instead of being encased. These one-handed clocks were introduced in 1720 and were still being made as late as 1778. Colonists also told time by the town clock, sundials, hourglasses, and watches.

THE SILVERSMITH/ THE APPRENTICE

The silversmith was the colonial banker. Colonists brought old English silver and coins to be transformed into teapots, trays, or bowls that could be marked and easily identified if stolen. Silver also came from the mines of Peru. In the North, foreign coins from pirates were an additional source of the precious metal. Boston led the colonial cities in the art of silversmithing before the Revolution, and a collection of the work of Paul Revere can be seen in the Boston Museum of Fine Arts today. Philadelphia and New York were known for having some outstanding craftsmen in silver. Silversmiths plied their trade in Charleston, Annapolis, and Williamsburg as well. Apprenticeships were an important part of the business.

GLOSSARY

apprentice—a person bound by a contract to work for another, usually an artisan, in return for learning a trade.

chamomile—an herb used to make a soothing tea.

Committee of Correspondence—The first Committee of Correspondence was organized by Samuel Adams in 1772 to connect the towns in Massachusetts and keep patriotism alive. Within a short time every colony except Pennsylvania had a similar group.

fripperies—fancy accessories sold in a shop.

hackle—a comb through which hair was passed when preparing it for a wig.

indenture—a contract between two people.

involuntary apprenticeships—apprenticeship of an orphan or poor person indentured to work for an artisan who did not have to train the apprentice in the trade, although most did.

journeyman—an apprentice who had served his term and not yet opened his own shop.

last—a wooden shape of a foot for a shoe.

limner—an itinerant painter of signs, portraits, clock faces.

mantua maker—a dressmaker who worked in a millinery shop or went from home to home fitting women for their gowns.

monopoly—exclusive control of a company or group of companies of the sale or production of an item or service.

peel—a wooden shovel used by the baker to shovel the loaves of bread into his oven.

Sons of Liberty—Patriots who were determined to advance the cause of American independence.

wag-on-the-wall—a one-handed clock mounted on a bracket with no case for the pendulum and weight works.

whispering sticks—a wooden object like a bit for a horse, put in a child's mouth and tied with strings in the back to prevent talking.

writing school—similar to an elementary school, where students learned reading, writing, spelling, arithmetic, and manners.

FURTHER READING

Barck, Oscar, and Hugh Lefler. *Colonial America*. New York: Macmillan Co., 1968.

*Bober, Natalie S. *Abigail Adams: Witness to a Revolution*. New York: Atheneum, 1995.

———. *Countdown to Independence: A Revolution of Ideas in England and Her American Colonies, 1760–1776*. New York: Atheneum, 2001.

Boston Weekly Gazette, December 23, 1773. #3664. Washington's Crossing, PA: David Library of the American Revolution.

Bridenbaugh, Carl. *The Colonial Craftsman*. New York: Dover, 1990.

*DePauw, Linda Grant. *Founding Mothers*. Boston: Houghton Mifflin, 1975. Reprint ed., 1994.

Earle, Alice Morse. *Child Life in Colonial Days*. Originally published 1899. Reprint ed., Stockbridge, MA: Berkshire House, 1993.

————. *Stage-Coach and Tavern Days*. New York: Macmillan Co., 1900. Reprint ed., New York: Dover, 1969.

*Fisher, Leonard Everett. *The Printers*. New York: Franklin Watts, 1965. Reissue, New York: Marshall Cavendish, 1990.

————. *The Schoolmasters*. New York: Franklin Watts, 1965. Reissue, New York: Marshall Cavendish, 1997.

————. *The Shoemakers*. New York: Franklin Watts, 1967. Reissue, New York: Marshall Cavendish, 1998.

————. *The Wigmakers*. New York: Franklin Watts, 1965. Reissue, New York: Marshall Cavendish, 2000.

Forbes, Esther. *Paul Revere and the World He Lived In*. Boston: Houghton Mifflin, 1942.

*Fritz, Jean. Ill., Tomie de Paola. *Can't You Make Them Behave, King George?* New York: Putnam, 1977. Reissue, 1996.

Gidwitz, Tom. "Freeing Captive History: The hunt for evidence of slavery in the North," *Archaeology*, Vol. 58, No. 2, (March/April 2005), pp.31–35.

Griswold, Wesley S. *The Boston Tea Party*. Kent, England: Abacus, 1972.

Hawke, David. *The Colonial Experience*. Indianapolis: Bobbs-Merrill, 1966.

*Hershenhorn, Esther. Ill., Megan Lloyd. *Fancy That*. New York: Holiday House, 2003.

*Hoose, Phillip. *We Were There, Too!: Young People in U.S. History*. New York: Farrar, Straus and Giroux, 2001.

*Katz, Susan. Ill., R.W. Alley. *A Revolutionary Field Trip: Poems of Colonial America*. New York: Simon and Schuster, 2004.

Labaree, Benjamin Woods. *The Boston Tea Party*. New York: Oxford University Press, 1964.

Lowance, Mason., ed. *Massachusetts Broadsides of the American Revolution*. Amherst, MA: University of Massachusetts Press, 1976.

Miller, John C. *Sam Adams*. Stanford, CA: Stanford University Press, 1936.

Norton, Mary Beth. *Liberty's Daughters: The Revolutionary Experience of American Women, 1750–1800*. Boston: Little, Brown, 1980; Ithaca, NY: Cornell University Press, 1996.

Randel, William Peirce. *The American Revolution: Mirror of a People*. Maplewood, NJ: Hammond, 1973.

Simmons, R. C. *The American Colonies: From Settlement to Independence*. New York: David McKay, 1976; Norton, 1980.

*Stevens, Bernardine. *Colonial American Craftspeople*. New York: Franklin Watts, 1993.

Tunis, Edwin. *Colonial Craftsmen: And the Beginnings of American Industry*. Cleveland and New York: World, 1965. Reprint ed., Baltimore, MD.: Johns Hopkins University Press, 1999.

Ulrich, Laurel Thatcher. *The Age of Homespun*. New York: Alfred Knopf, 2001.

————. *A Midwife's Tale*. New York: Random House, 1990.

Vaughan, Alden. *America Before the Revolution, 1725–1775*. Englewood Cliffs, NJ: Prentice Hall, 1967.

Walker, Niki, and Bobbie Kalman. *The Milliner*. New York: Crabtree, 2002.

Wall, C. A. *The Historic Boston Tea Party*. Worcester, MA: Blanchard & Co., 1896.

Washburn, Wilcomb. *Indians and the American Revolution*. www.americanrevolution.org.

*Winslow, Anna Green. *Diary of Anna Green Winslow: A Boston School Girl of 1771*. Boston: Houghton Mifflin, 1894. Reprint ed. Bedford, MA: Applewood Books, 1997.

* Indicates books students might enjoy.

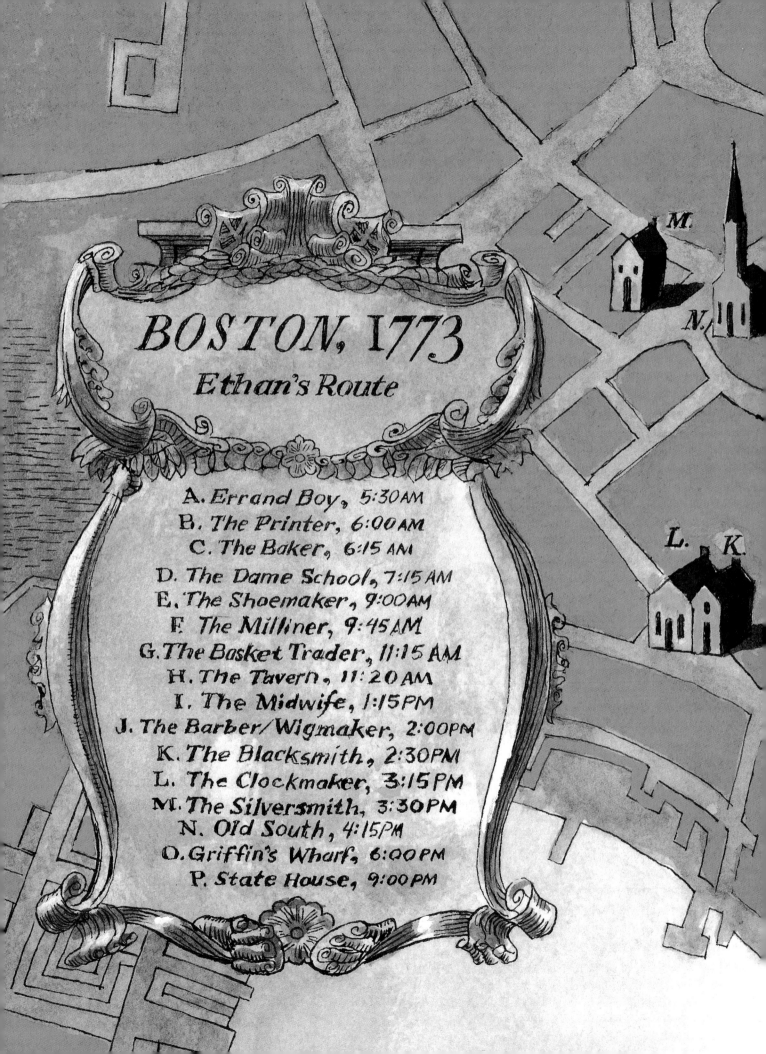

BOOKS BY KAY WINTERS

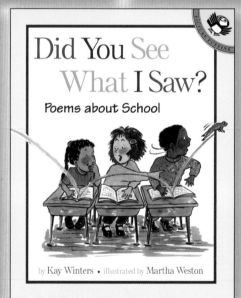